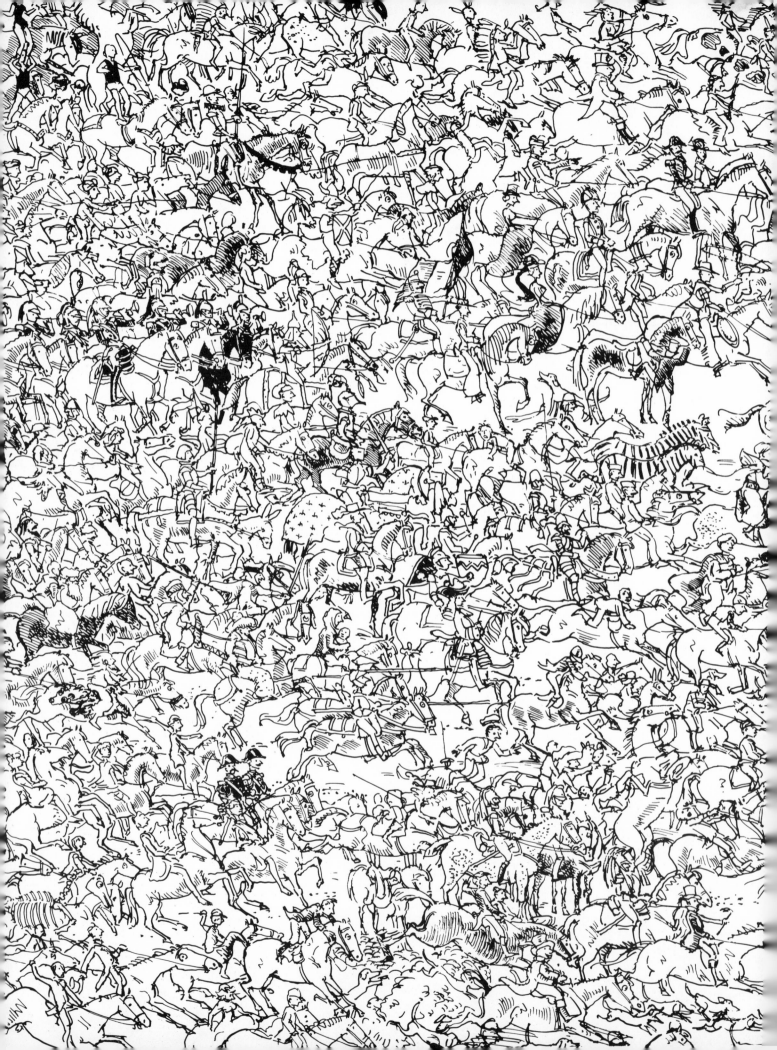

Dedicated to Colonel E.L.
with my thanks

Whenever I had trouble explaining a movement or position,
I consulted the works of General Decarpentry,
the foremost authority in matters of horsemanship,
and borrowed what I needed.

Prentice-Hall International, Inc., London
Prentice-Hall of Australia, Pty. Ltd., North Sydney
Prentice-Hall of Canada, Ltd., Toronto
Prentice-Hall of India Private Ltd., New Delhi
Prentice-Hall of Japan, Inc., Tokyo
Prentice-Hall of Southeast Asia Pte. Ltd., Singapore
Whitehall Books Limited, Wellington, New Zealand

10 9 8 7 6 5 4 3 2 1

Library of Congress Cataloging in Publication Data
Dumas, Philippe.   The Lippizaners.
Translation of L'équitation et l'Ecole espagnole de Vienne.
SUMMARY: Discusses the Spanish Riding School of
Vienna where the Lippizaners are trained and this
special horse breed, famous throughout the world.
1. Lippizaner horse–Juvenile literature. 2. Vienna.
Spanische Reitschule–Juvenile literature.
3. Dressage–Juvenile literature. 4. Horses–
Juvenile literature. [1. Lippizaner horse.
2. Vienna. Spanische Reitschule. 3. Horses.]I. Title.
SF293. L5D8513   1981   798.2'4'0943613
80-26008   ISBN 0-13-537068-X

Philippe Dumas

THE LIPPIZANERS
and the Spanish Riding School of Vienna

Illustrated by the author
Translated by Mariana Fitzpatrick

Prentice-Hall Inc., Englewood Cliffs, N.J.

preface

The dapple gray hobbyhorse with its black mane is no longer found in toy stores. It has been replaced by the warm flesh of real ponies. The beloved wooden steed, prized by a generation weaned on hoofbeats and rumbling carriages, that faithful companion to whom childhood secrets were whispered while rocking from bedroom to kitchen, has come alive. He needs space to trot and canter. He blinks his eyes. He whinnies and tosses his mane. Along with his larger cousins, he has a new relationship with man. No longer an indispensable working companion, he contributes richly to our leisure hours, our physical well-being, and our cultural life. Available to many and familiar to all (thanks to television, films and literature), he fulfills a need which lies deep in our history. This book by Philippe Dumas opens doors for young and old alike, demonstrating that horsemanship is not an end in itself. It is a search to be undertaken, a concept to be fathomed, a body of work to ponder.

Laurent Cresp
Technical Advisor to the
Pony Club of France

I think that I've always loved horses.
I was born in 1940, during the war.
France was occupied by enemy troops.
It was hard to find gasoline.
Some handy people converted their cars to run on bottled gas.
Others used charcoal for fuel.
Since the automobile was a fairly recent invention,
garages were packed with carriages in good condition.
As these returned to the streets,
Paris filled up with horses.

I remember
the moving men's
long, sideless wagons
drawn by white Percherons.
I remember
carts from the *Glacières de Paris*
delivering chunks of ice
to our grocer, Monsieur Mantot.
I can still see the milkman's team
and the ragman's pony.
There were carts, gigs and coaches
everywhere.
Even proud thoroughbreds
were forced into harness.
Those with the money
took carriages now in place of taxis.
I loved the sound
of hoofbeats in the street,
especially the clip-clopping
over wooden paving blocks.

Along the Avenue Malakoff, coachmen fed their charges while waiting for fares.
The beasts made me laugh with their feedbags on their heads.
One day I stroked the neck
of a powerful animal who was hitched to half a car.
The owner had cut off
the front wheels and engine
and replaced them with a horse.

On a cold winter evening, I peered out the dining room window
and saw a horse sprawled in his traces at the end of our narrow street.
The animal thrashed about. He tried to roll over.
"A bad case of colic," said my brother Jean-Louis.
Bystanders stood and gaped.
The coachman covered the beast with a blanket, then attempted to help him stand.
We were called to the table. When I returned to the window,
there was nothing left to see. The roadway was deserted.

After the war, carriages disappeared. Noisy smelly engines
took over the streets again. I was so young
that I thought motorcars were a brand-new invention.

True, the Dumesnil Beer cart
still racketed down the Rue Franklin,
delivering its wares in a clatter of trotting hooves.
And once a week the Garde Républicaine crossed Paris
on their way to the Longchamps Race Track and back.
However, you had to know precisely where they'd be passing.
We usually settled for the same lone soldier
posting along the Avenue Henri Martin toward the Bois de Boulogne,
leading his officer's mount.
But sights such as these grew rare and I sensed that
one of Paris's pleasures was coming to an end.

Mademoiselle Muños on Moustache

MANÈGE

Monsieur Fromageot

The riding master

Soon only a few riding schools
remained.
(They're gone today,
replaced by
department stores
and apartment buildings.)
Children, stout women
and stern-faced men
flocked there
to learn horsemanship.
There was a riding school near my house.
I'd drop by after classes
to watch the riders.

Monsieur Lamare

Right leg,
left hand
and into
the canter!

A friendly stableboy
taught me the horses' names: the roan mare Désirée,
sturdy Blue Boy, bad-tempered Tango and the others.
My brother Olivier spent his allowance
on weekly riding lessons. I'd tag along
and watch from the gallery.
He got terrible scoldings from the riding master
Monsieur Laurent,
but that didn't spoil our fun.
It was here that I saw
my cousin Isaline take a nasty fall in the ring.
During the bike ride home, my brother showed me
how to handle a horse.

Naturally I dreamed of riding someday.
I practiced as best I could,
first on farm animals,
later on donkeys in the amusement park.
But my father found my taste for horses "snobbish"
and refused to encourage me.
I didn't begin riding seriously until I was fifteen.
But I've made up for lost time since
and I don't plan to stop now
despite my advanced age.

To simply say we ride doesn't mean much.
Anyone can get on a horse:
cowboys in films, children in the park,
farmers going to market, vacationers at the Club Méditerranée.
But over the centuries, after long and careful thought, certain horsemen
have transformed the act of riding into a true art and what I dare call
a philosophy.
Man has been dreaming of mastering horses since ancient times.
Xenophon, Socrates's disciple, left us two works on the subject,
full of wise and subtle sayings.

Classical horsemanship reached its height
in 18th-century France.
A horsemaster named François de La Guérinière
(1687-1751)
has surely never
been surpassed.
Remember that in those days,
knowing how to sit
on an able obedient horse
could mean the difference between life and death!
Everything took place on horseback,
especially warfare.
Charging the enemy,
wheeling away from blows,
driving one's weapon home,
and if needed,

François Robichon de la
Guérinière

retreating,
required mastering the science of riding
as thoroughly as pilots today
must master mathematics in order to fly
a Concorde.

Hermès   Louis XIII   Antoine de Pluvinel

Tapestry in the Kunst Historisches Museum
in Vienna, from a sketch by the painter Jordaens.

The future King Louis XIII studied horsemanship with Pluvinel
as seriously as political science is studied today
by people who hope to be president.
La Guérinière's artistry was the highest flowering
of a long French tradition which continued
until the French Revolution when the riding schools were
closed, disbanded and dispersed.
The Riding School at Versailles was reopened under the Restoration
but it disappeared forever in 1830.
Since Saumur, the French cavalry school, is basically a military institution,
it has not preserved the secrets of classical horsemanship
in their purest form.

Some horsemen today,
including Nuno Oliveira and his students,
still look to La Guérinière and try to follow his teachings
which have been perfected by the later findings of experts
like Baucher (1796-1873), a rider of true genius.

La Guérinière

François Baucher

Nuno Oliveira
on Saturno

The classical tradition lives on in Austria's Spanish School (*Spanische Schule*)
which has survived every war and change in government since its founding
in 1729. Established fifty years after the riding school at Versailles,
it struggled to rival the French in the application of principles
taught by La Guérinière in his "Cavalry School."
World famous today, Vienna's Spanish Riding School
was named for the birthplace of its horses,
Spanish blood being highly prized in the 18th century.

On a trip to Austria
my family and I had the privilege of visiting the famous school.
Try to imagine a huge building right in the midst of the city,
a place which looks like anything but a lodging for horses.
It's part of the Hofburg Palace.
The imposing entrance quickly cuts newcomers down to size.

My wife and I were greeted
by a severe-looking officer who showed us to the gallery.
It was still rather early in the day.
Alone in the ring, beneath magnificent chandeliers,
an elderly rider was working his horse in absolute silence.

We were struck by the solemnity
of our surroundings.
In this temple of horsemanship,
the aging rider
on his steed
practicing high school dressage
seemed to
glorify
knowledge gained
as it is given.

Like all arts horsemanship is practiced well

badly

with genius

routinely

Horsemanship has little to do
with galloping down the beach
hooting and shouting.
It's a philosophy
as I've said before,
or if you prefer,
a kind of moral schooling.
It teaches us to be relaxed yet energetic,
active yet calm,
gentle yet forceful,
respectful yet firm,
flexible yet effective,
trusting yet watchful,
and careful in all things.
It's hard not to dream
of a new School of Versailles
conceived
in the great French tradition
with all its brilliance.
But let's not cry over the past.
Instead let's examine this Viennese School
which restores some of the teachings
of earlier days.

the horses

Vienna's Spanish Riding School is above all a special breed of horses:
the Lippizan or Lippizaner.
These magnificent animals are descended from stallions and mares
purchased in Andalusia at the start of the 18th century and selectively bred
over more than two hundred years for
gentleness and schooling ability.
From the early 1700's until World War I
the horses were raised on the Lippiza Stud Farm
in a village which is now part of Yugoslavia but which once belonged to
the Austrian Empire.
It was here that the Lippizaner developed as a breed,
basically Spanish in origin
with occasional additions of Arab and Neapolitan blood.

*Foals are born with dark coats (bay, deep brown
and dark gray). These lighten with the years, gradually
becoming pure white.*

All "true" Lippizaners belong to one of six dynasties whose founding sires are:
Pluto (white), Spanish, born at the Danish Royal Stud Farm in 1765;
Conversano (black), Neapolitan, born in 1767;
Napolitano (bay), Neapolitan, born in 1790;
Favory (dun), Andalusian, born in Lippiza in 1779;
Maestoso (white), Andalusian, born in 1819;
Siglavy (white), Arab, born in Syria in 1810.

At the end of World War I, the stud farm was moved to
the Austrian village of Piber in Styria.
"The Lippizaner is marked by his strong frame,
rather short height (15 to 15.3 hands) and noble bearing.
His neck is often arched,
his eyes are remarkably expressive,
his ears well set. His withers are somewhat pronounced,
his back rather long, his flanks perfectly positioned.
His rump is strongly muscled and rounded, his legs extremely strong,
his feet well-turned.
The Lippizaner is known above all else for
his sterling character."

As the fighting approached Vienna during World War II,
the Riding Masters asked General Patton,
who had studied at Saumur,
for his protection.
He arranged for the entire operation
(stallions, mares, foals, even the equipment)
to be moved by truck
to a safer place.

the stables

The stables, situated on the ground floor of the Stallburg
with its arcaded Renaissance courtyard,
are connected to the Riding Hall by the arched Burgtor.
Each autumn,
a new group of stallions arrives in Vienna
to join the school horses in the Spanish Riding School and begin their education.
Although they are already four years old,
their first two years of training
are limited to a "slow and careful" breaking in.

On arrival the stallions are placed in stalls.
Stone horseheads, positioned between each window,
gaze unblinkingly down
at the animals eating their oats
from red marble mangers.
A decorative marble border runs the length
of the stable.

wood

33

A Lippizan from Piber is branded with an L on the left cheek
and a P topped with a crown on the left hip.
The initial of his founding sire appears on his barrel under the saddle place.

Sired by a descendant of

P	Pluto
C	Conversano
N	Napolitano
F	Favory
M	Maestoso
S	Siglavy

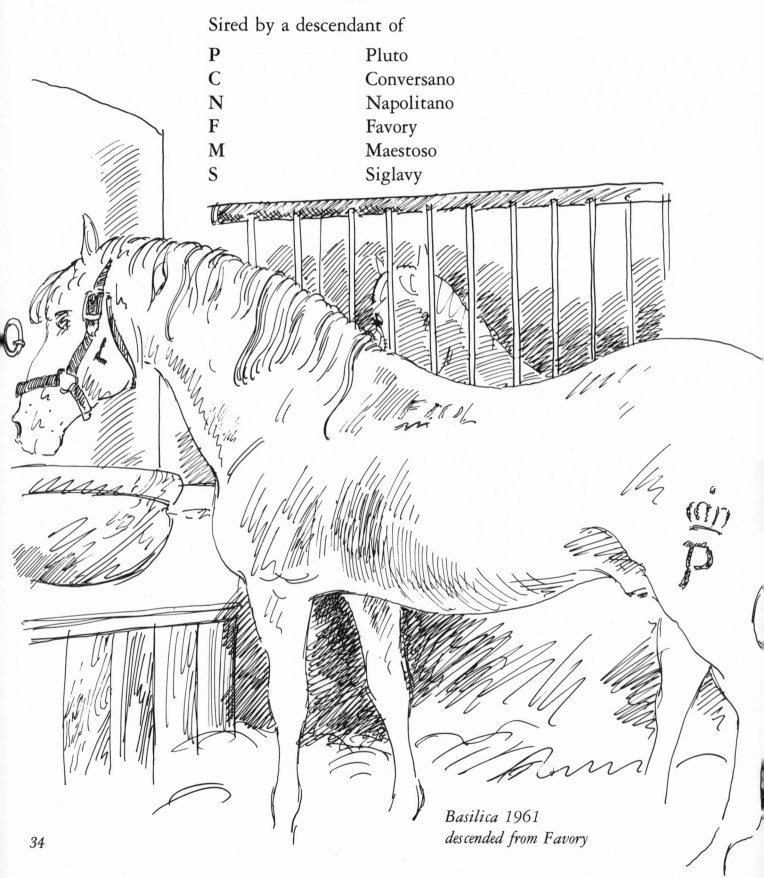

Basilica 1961
descended from Favory

*carved headpiece
of saddle rack*

Saddles are stored in layers.
A special forked pole is used
to reach the top rows.

Vienna's Spanish Riding School provides a remarkable setting.
Its luxurious Riding Hall, bathed in light,
looks more like a drawing room or reception hall
than an exercise ring. Frenchmen recall with pride
that its Austrian architect, Fischer von Erlach,
relied almost completely on plans
drawn up by Mansart for the chapel at Versailles.

Except for the riders' gold-buttoned brown frock coats,
the carefully raked red sawdust on the ground
and the scarlet velvet gallery railings,
the breathtaking Riding Hall is completely white.

A painting of Emperor Charles VI who founded the Riding School
hangs in the Imperial Box facing the entrance.
"Riders entering the Hall
must immediately track to the right,
rein up before the Emperor's portrait
and give the traditional salute."

The Riding Hall, fifty-five meters long
by eighteen meters wide,
is surrounded by 46 Corinthian columns
that support the upper gallery.
Begun in 1729,
the winter Riding Hall was completed in 1735.

trapping and dress

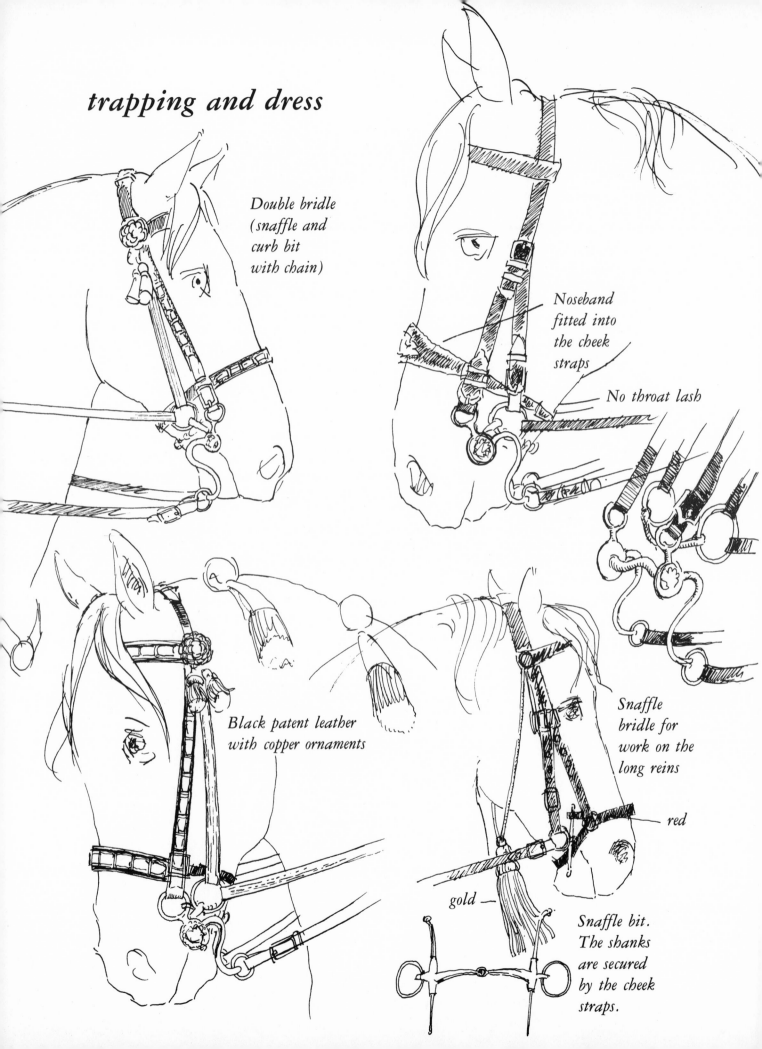

Double bridle
(snaffle and
curb bit
with chain)

Noseband
fitted into
the cheek
straps

No throat lash

Black patent leather
with copper ornaments

Snaffle
bridle for
work on the
long reins

red

gold

Snaffle bit.
The shanks
are secured
by the cheek
straps.

show saddle

Traditional white deerskin saddle, built up at the pommel and cantle.

Black two-cornered hat

Chestnut brown frock coat buttoned to the throat.

Red saddle pad used with gold bridle. Green saddle pad used with black bridle.

Saddle pad trimmed with gold in accordance with the rider's rank

white gloves

buckskin breeches

high, polished boots

simple birch switch

curved spurs

the gaits

work at the walk	the walk (four-beat gait)	the rein back	(backward movement made up of diagonal thrusts)
work at the trot	the working trot	the passage	the piaffe (passage in place)
work at the canter	the canter	the hand gallop (controlled and collected gallop)	the "terre à terre" (high-stepping canter done almost in place) the "mezair" (short series of levades during which the forehand only touches the ground for an instant)
two-tracking (side-stepping)	the shoulder-in (the horse's body is bent toward the rider's inside leg)	the traversal (the horse's body is parallel to the long wall of the arena)	the shoulder-out (the horse's body is bent toward the rider's outside leg)
pirouettes	pirouettes at the canter (the haunches serve as a pivot for the rest of the body)	the pirouette in the piaffe	

the airs above the ground or "school jumps"	18th-century French School	Viennese School	School of Saumur

the airs
above the ground
or "school jumps"
"stylized forms of the natural leaps of horses running free"

18th-century French School
(from engravings by Charles Parrocel)

Viennese School

School of Saumur

the courbette
the horse springs up almost vertically without touching his forelegs to the ground

the levade
the haunches are deeply bent and the forehand raised lightly not as high as in the "pesade haute")

Above
A courbette in the style of Saumur (actually a rear performed on demand)

the croupade
the horse thrusts himself forward and upward, back legs tucked beneath him

the ballotade
the horse thrusts himself forward and upward, showing his shoes

Above
A croupade in the style of Saumur: the horse lashes out from the halt, braced on the forehand (This is not a classical exercise and is therefore not practiced in Vienna. It is actually a buck performed on demand.)

the capriole
in the capriole the rider attempts to make the horse lash out with his hind feet at the instant that the forehand reaches its highest point of elevation

trot, passage, piaffe

trot

passage

instant when all four feet leave the earth

"In this highly stylized trot, the horse concentrates on springing upwards with each step, seeming barely to skim the ground."

piaffe

"Rather than thrusting forward, the hooves move up and down, as the horse trots lightly in place."

work on the longeing rein

The longeing rein is used chiefly to break in horses.
As the colt gains strength, he begins lessons
on the longeing rein. These training sessions are gradually lengthened.
The rider's first aim is to accustom the horse to his weight
and to gain the animal's confidence through
voice and caresses, never touching the reins
at first, later holding them
as evenly and lightly as possible.
When the horse performs well on the longeing rein
and can be easily collected,
he is ready to move on to more advanced work
"in hand."

The Ballotade
*The longeing rein
measuring 6 or 8
meters is attached
to a ring in the
cavecon.*

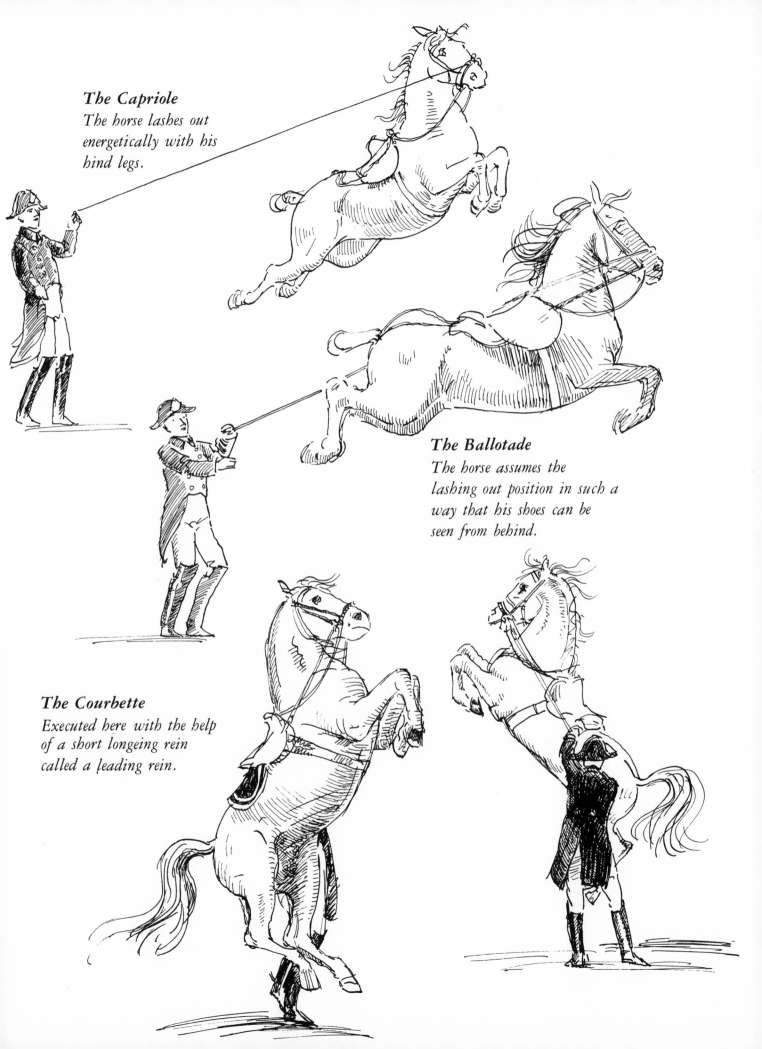

The Capriole
The horse lashes out energetically with his hind legs.

The Ballotade
The horse assumes the lashing out position in such a way that his shoes can be seen from behind.

The Courbette
Executed here with the help of a short longeing rein called a leading rein.

work on the ground

The horse pictured here is learning to piaffe.
"After positioning the horse parallel to the wall,
the horseman stands at the animal's shoulder,
controlling him with a shortened longeing rein.
The horse is gradually collected at the walk
with the help of taps from a long whip or switch
on the hindquarters until he moves into
an easily maintained slow and rhythmic trot.
The trot is gradually slowed
until it is practically executed in place.
The piaffe is never asked for
directly from a halt."

*The levade or pesade
in hand, an exercise
that evolved from
the piaffe.*

46

*His hocks deeply bent,
the horse puts his full weight on his hindquarters.*

*This sketch shows the progressive collection of the hindquarters during
preparation for high school dressage.*

work on the long reins

"The highly trained horse
executes all the gaits and airs
guided by long reins alone
with a little discreet help
from the whip."
These horses are so gentle
that the Riding Masters stand
either flush with their haunches
or directly behind the rump.

gold

red

Monsieur Irbinger conducts a passage on the long reins.
The Riding Masters attach the guide reins directly to the bit
without passing them through rings in the collar or surcingle.

At right:
The arrangement of
the long reins
recommended by
General Decarpentry
facilitates work
on the circle.

work between the pillars

"This work is not begun until the second year of training.
It starts with the piaffe in hand (on an unmounted horse).
If the animal seems gifted, he is put between the pillars.
His behavior there usually indicates
whether he has the aptitude necessary to perform the high school figures."

the piaffe

*Don't be surprised by this bay stallion.
The Spanish Riding School
traditionally contains
one dark-coated horse.*

*The levade. The horse holds this
position for several moments.*

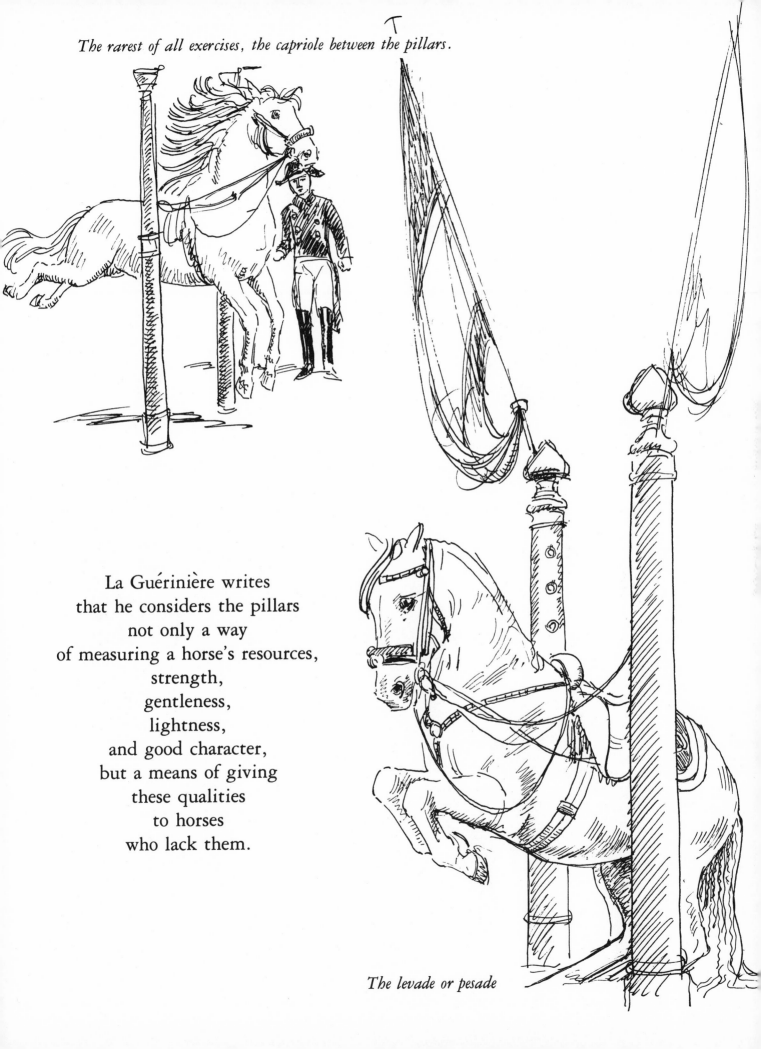

The rarest of all exercises, the capriole between the pillars.

La Guérinière writes
that he considers the pillars
not only a way
of measuring a horse's resources,
strength,
gentleness,
lightness,
and good character,
but a means of giving
these qualities
to horses
who lack them.

The levade or pesade

work under saddle

The two drawings below show the difference in style
between the French and Austrian schools.
To the left: School of Saumur—reins loose, chin tucked, neck high.
The horse is light and brilliant.
To the right: School of Vienna—the reins are tighter.
The horse is extremely obedient but not as light.

*The passage (General Wattel, on Rampart),
Head Riding Master of the "cadre noir"
during the School of Saumur's most
brilliant period.*

The passage (Riding Master Gebhardt)

*Notice the flexibility of
the fetlock joint.*

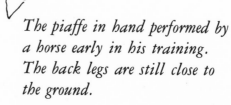

*The piaffe in hand performed by
a horse early in his training.
The back legs are still close to
the ground.*

The piaffe. The hind legs are strongly collected under the hindquarters. Notice the flexibility of the forehand.

Two handsome passages. As the horse proceeds, chin tucked, neck high, his back legs vibrate.

pirouettes

In the pirouette
the horse's hindquarters or, more exactly,
one hind leg
serves as a pivot for the rest of the body.
The forehand
traces a circle around this rear leg.
This is one of the most beautiful
high school figures. The horse seems to
dance in place.

*A pirouette
from a painting
by G. Hamilton
(18th Century).*

*Pirouette to the right
from a drawing by
Parrocel for a
book by La Guérinière.*

the pirouette on the hindquarters

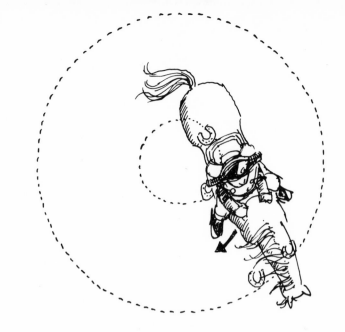

A pirouette as performed in Vienna today.

Riding Master Lindenbauer executes a pirouette to the left.

school jumps

Remember that these are
stylized versions
of the natural leaps of horses
running free.

*The levade
normally executed
by guardians in the
Camargue is
identical to the
levade practiced
at Saumur as
the "Courbette."*

*His full weight on his hindquarters,
the horse raises his forehand,
hocks deeply bent.*

*The pesade haute.
The hocks are
not as flexed as
in the ordinary
pesade.*

the capriole

"Vienna's Riding Masters strive to make their horses
kick out energetically with both hind legs as the
forequarters reach maximum height, in order for the horse
to return to the ground on all four feet."

the courbette

This breakdown of the courbette shows how
the horse
in the pesade position
thrusts off from his hind legs into the air,
then returns to the pesade position.

courbettes
(in the saddle or on the ground)

These are undoubtedly the most difficult and spectacular jumps
performed in Vienna.
There is nothing more impressive than the sight of a stallion
erect on his hind legs, leaping forward again and again,
sometimes as many as ten times.

We've arrived at the end of our story.
Those of you who like
to ride for pleasure
and sometimes exercise in the ring
may think that the time and patience
it takes for these expert horsemen
to achieve even the smallest improvement
is pointless and has nothing to do with you.

Yet . . . although horsemanship is fun,
the very joy it brings makes it an art as well.
And, as with all the arts,
there is constant progress to make and more to learn every day
until you are very old.
In his memoirs, General L'Hotte writes
that for more than sixty years
he seldom got off a horse
without wanting to jot down the thoughts inspired
by a "chat with his dearest friend."
If horses no longer serve as they did to transport us,
they remain incomparable tools in our search for self-knowledge.
One of man's oldest dreams is to link his mind with the horse's strong body.

A centaur would be born of this union.
But to become a centaur,
flesh and spirit must be mastered in harmony.
In the 18th century, one of France's great nobles
brought his son to Monsieur Duplessis.
"I don't want you to make my boy a great rider," he explained.
"I'd simply like you to
attune his arms and legs
to what his mind wants his horse to perform."
"My lord," Duplessis replied, "I've been working to learn what I teach
for some sixty years.
What you're asking is precisely what I'd most like to know how to do."
If we reflect on the old master's words,
we see that high school horsemanship
is a kind of philosophy
which requires absolute concentration.
It's an art closer to Zen than to sports . . .
but for now, have a good gallop. See you later!

Author-horseman tumbles from his chair

about the author

Philippe Dumas is a prize-winning illustrator who was awarded the "Prix Graphique" in 1977 for THE STORY OF EDWARD and named by *The New York Times* as one of the ten best illustrators of 1978 for ODETTE: *A Bird in Paris.* His other children's books include CAESAR: *Cock of the Village,* selected for the "Beaux Livres de l'Année" 1978, and LUCIE: *A Tale of a Donkey,* all published by Prentice-Hall. Mr. Dumas lives with his wife, Kay Fender, and his three young children in Fontaine-le-Dun, France.

about the translator

Mariana Fitzpatrick, an editor and translator, and her daughters Susan and Jessica spent happy years on horseback in France in the ring at the Centre Equestre de Maurepas outside of Paris and on the white horses of the Camargue.

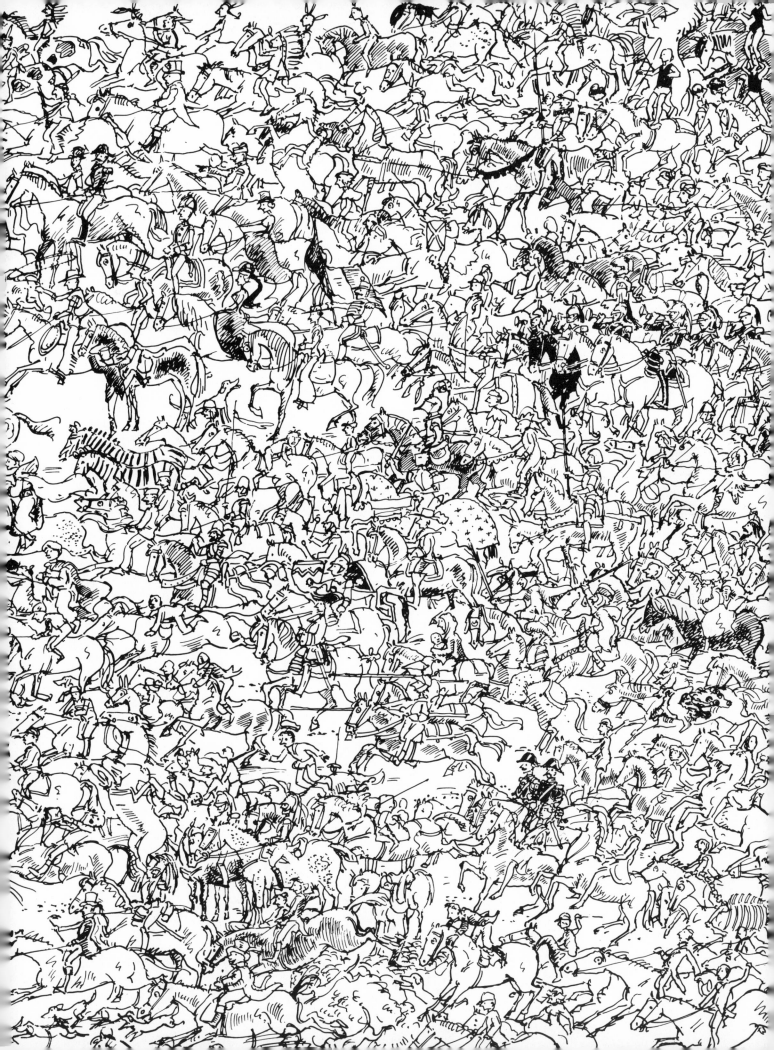

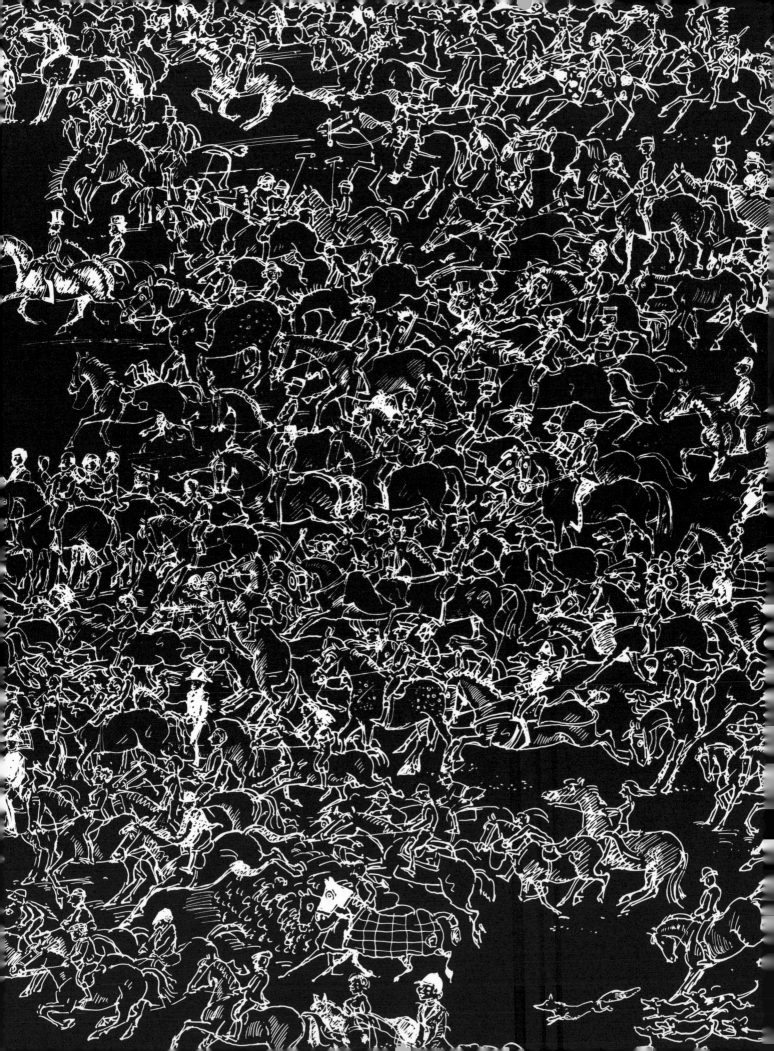